3-3

Sound
Loud, Soft, High, and Low

Written by Natalie M. Rosinsky
Illustrated by Matthew John

Content Advisor: Dr. Paul Ohmann, Assistant Professor of Physics, University of St. Thomas, St. Paul, Minnesota
Reading Advisor: Lauren A. Liang, M.A., Literacy Education, University of Minnesota, Minneapolis, Minnesota

AMAZING SCIENCE

PICTURE WINDOW BOOKS
MINNEAPOLIS, MINNESOTA

Editor: Nadia Higgins
Designer: Melissa Voda
Page production: The Design Lab
The illustrations in this book were prepared digitally.

PICTURE WINDOW BOOKS
5115 Excelsior Boulevard
Suite 232
Minneapolis, MN 55416
1-877-845-8392
www.picturewindowbooks.com

Printed in the United States of America.
1 2 3 4 5 6 08 07 06 05 04 03

Library of Congress Cataloging-in-Publication Data
Rosinsky, Natalie M. (Natalie Myra)
  Sound : loud, soft, high, and low / written by Natalie M.
Rosinsky ; illustrated by Matthew John.
    p. cm. — (Amazing science) Includes bibliographical
references and index.
  ISBN 1-4048-0016-6 (lib. bdg. : alk. paper)
  1. Sound—Juvenile literature. [1. Sound.] I. John,
Matthew, ill. II. Title.
  QC225.5 .R67 2003
  534—dc21   2002005740

TABLE OF CONTENTS

How Are Sounds Made?

A baseball smacks against
a wooden bat. Thwack!

Raindrops tap against your window. Pitter patter, pitter patter. How are sounds made?

Tap a musical triangle.
You can see it shake.

As the triangle vibrates,
it makes sound. Sound is
made from vibrating things.

Fun fact: When you talk, the vocal chords inside your throat vibrate. Place your hands firmly on the middle of your throat. Now hum. Do you feel your vocal chords flutter?

Throw a pebble into a pond. Watch how the ripples move away from the splash. Sound moves in waves like ripples in the pond.

Sound waves move in all directions from a baseball bat, a raindrop, or anything else that makes sound. The waves travel through the air to your ears, but you can't see them. Sound waves are invisible.

Fun fact: Sound waves travel through water, too.
Whales and dolphins hear sound waves in the ocean.

What Makes an Echo?

Stand inside a big, empty room. Now, shout your name. It sounds as if someone is saying your name back at you. You have made an echo.

Echoes are made when sound waves bounce off big, hard things like walls or mountains. When the sound bounces back to you, you hear it again.

Fun fact: Bats use echoes to find their way through dark caves. As the bats fly about, they make squeaky sounds. They listen for echoes to tell them where the cave walls are.

Why Are Some Sounds Loud and Others Soft?

If you throw a pebble hard into the water, it makes big waves that travel far. When you bang a drum hard, the drum booms loudly. It makes big sound waves that travel far.

If you tap the drum lightly, it rumbles softly. The sound waves are smaller and do not go as far.

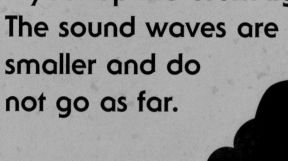

Be careful! Loud sounds from music or noisy machines can hurt your ears.

Sometimes a sound is loud because you are close to it. A whisper can be loud and clear, if your friend is standing next to you.

Why Are Some Sounds High and Others Low?

Pluck the thinnest, tightest string on a guitar. You can see it vibrate very quickly. Listen to the sound it makes. Things that vibrate quickly make high-pitched sounds.

Fun fact: Some sounds are too high for people to hear. A dog can hear high noises that seem like silence to us.

Sometimes people say, "Turn down the volume!"
That means they want the sound softened.
Volume is another word for loudness.

Fun fact: Builders think about sound when they
plan buildings. Some places, like libraries and
hospitals, are made to be quiet. Other places,
like concert halls, are built so sound resounds.

17

Sometimes people say, "Turn down the volume!"
That means they want the sound softened.
Volume is another word for loudness.

Fun fact: Builders think about sound when they
plan buildings. Some places, like libraries and
hospitals, are made to be quiet. Other places,
like concert halls, are built so sound resounds.

Why Are Some Sounds High and Others Low?

Pluck the thinnest, tightest string on a guitar. You can see it vibrate very quickly. Listen to the sound it makes. Things that vibrate quickly make high-pitched sounds.

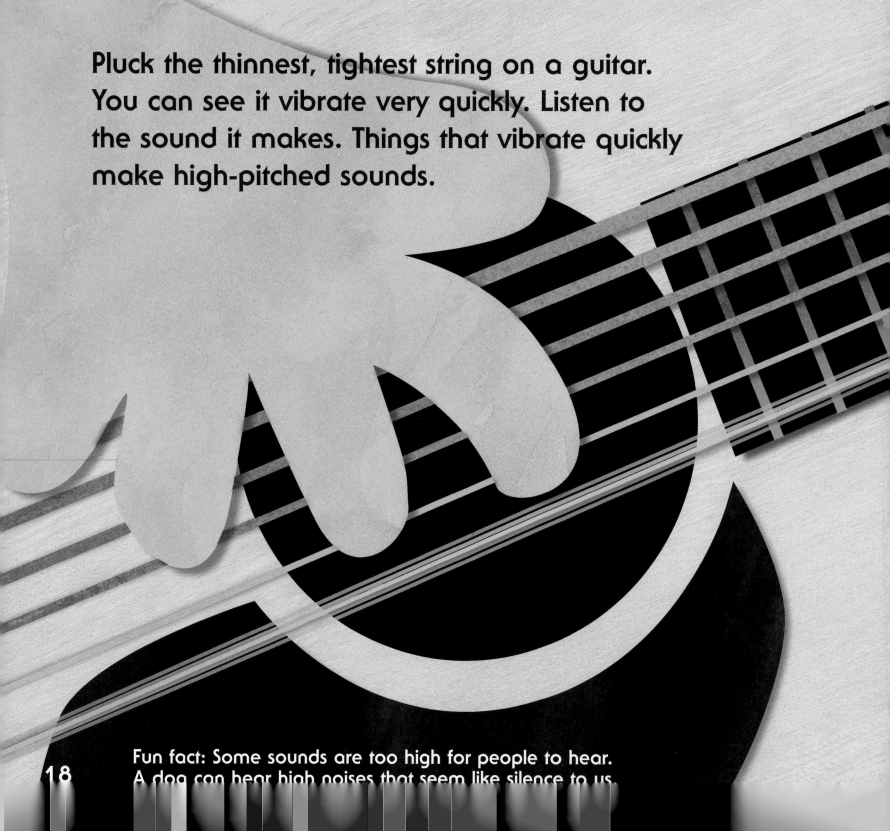

Fun fact: Some sounds are too high for people to hear. A dog can hear high noises that seem like silence to us.

You can make a sound seem softer or louder. Put your hands over your ears, and a sound seems softer. Cup your hands around your ears, and you can catch more sound waves. The sound seems louder.

The roar of an airplane sounds soft
when it is far up in the sky.

Loud sounds are sometimes helpful.
Alarm clocks buzz and wake us up.
Sirens yell when danger is near.

15

The thickest string on a guitar vibrates more slowly. It makes a low-pitched sound.

Now you know all about sound—loud, soft, high, and low. What kinds of sounds can *you* make?

What's the highest sound you've ever heard? What's the lowest? What are the loudest and the softest sounds you can think of?

21

Experiments

Make Musical Glasses: Take three tall drinking glasses. Fill up the first glass until it's almost full. Fill up the second glass so that the water level is one inch ($2\frac{1}{2}$ centimeters) lower than the water in the first glass. Fill up the third glass so that the water is one inch ($2\frac{1}{2}$ centimeters) lower than in the second. Tap the top of each glass with a pencil.

Which glass makes the highest sound? Which one makes the lowest sound? Do glasses vibrate faster when they are empty or full?

Make a Sound Softer: Strike a metal fork with a metal spoon. Listen to the sounds the fork's teeth make as they vibrate. Now place pieces of cotton between the fork's teeth. Strike the fork with the spoon again. What do you hear now?

Fast Facts: Hearing Sound, Feeling Sound

Getting an Earful: An eardrum is a piece of tight, thin skin that's stretched inside your ear. The drum is about the size of the tip of your finger. When sound hits your eardrum, it vibrates. The eardrum helps carry the sound into the inside part of your ear and to your brain. Your brain figures out if the sound is loud or soft, high or low.

Ear Times Two: Having an ear on each side of your head helps you find out where a sound comes from. A sound reaches the ear that's closer to it faster than it reaches the other ear. The sound seems louder to the closer ear. Having two ears helps you know where to look when someone calls your name.

Bone-Shaking Sound: Sound travels through your bones. At a loud concert, you can feel the booming of a drumbeat through your whole body.

Who Was *That?* Are you surprised by the sound of your own voice on a tape recording? The recording is what you sound like to other people as your voice reaches them through the air. You hear your own voice as it vibrates through the bones of your head.

Glossary

eardrum—a thin layer of skin inside the ear that vibrates when sound waves hit it

echo—a sound that is repeated. Echoes are made when sound waves bounce off big, hard things and come back to you.

pitch—how high or low a sound is

vibrate—a small but quick movement back and forth. Vibrations make sounds.

vocal chords—the part of a person's or animal's throat that vibrates to make sound. Vocal chords let people talk.

volume—how loud or soft a sound is

To Learn More

At the Library

Hewitt, Sally. *Hearing Sounds.* New York: Children's Press, 1998.

Pfeffer, Wendy. *Sounds All Around.* New York: HarperCollins, 1999.

Stille, Darlene R. *Sound.* Mankato, Minn.: Compass Point Books, 2001.

On the Web

ThinkQuest
http://www.thinkquest.org
For science information and links

National Geographic
http://www.nationalgeographic.com
For science information

Want to learn more about sound? Visit FACT HOUND at *http://www.facthound.com.*

Index